contents

strawberry porridge 4
french toast 7
buttermilk pancakes with
  strawberries 8
pancakes with maple cream 11
cheesy breakfast rolls 12
ham & cheese scrolls 15
choc-chip pikelets 16
breakfast pizzas 19

breakfasts

strawberry porridge

serves 4
preparation 3 minutes
cooking 10 minutes

4 cups (1 litre) milk, plus extra to serve
  (optional)
1½ cups (135g) rolled oats
2 punnets strawberries, hulled, quartered
1 tablespoon cinnamon sugar

step 1 In a saucepan, combine milk and oats.
Bring to the boil over a medium heat, stirring
constantly.
step 2 Reduce the heat to low. Stir in
strawberries. Simmer for 5-10 minutes, stirring
occasionally, until strawberries are cooked to
your liking. Remove from heat.
step 3 Spoon into 4 bowls. Sprinkle evenly
with cinnamon sugar. Pour over extra milk,
if using, to serve.

tips You can use brown sugar in place of the
cinnamon sugar, if you like.

french toast

serves 4
preparation 5 minutes
cooking 5 minutes

2 eggs
½ cup (125ml) cream or milk
1 tablespoon sugar
½ teaspoon ground cinnamon
4 thick slices brioche (or other bread)
15g butter
icing sugar, to dust
mixed berries, maple syrup, to serve

step 1 Place eggs, cream or milk, sugar and cinnamon in a shallow bowl. Whisk to combine.
step 2 Soak brioche in egg mixture for a few seconds each side.
step 3 Heat the butter in a frying pan on medium heat. When the butter is foaming, place the soaked brioche slices in the frying pan. Cook for 2-3 minutes each side or until golden. Dust with icing sugar, top with berries and drizzle with maple syrup.

tip This is also delicious served with crispy bacon, roasted tomatoes and sautéed mushrooms. Just omit the icing sugar, maple syrup and berries.

buttermilk pancakes with strawberries

makes 16
preparation 10 minutes (plus standing time)
cooking 20 minutes

2 cups (300g) self-raising flour, sifted
⅓ cup (75g) caster sugar
2⅓ cups (580ml) buttermilk
2 eggs, lightly beaten
50g butter, melted
1 teaspoon vanilla extract
2 punnets strawberries, washed and hulled
icing sugar, to serve

step 1 In a large bowl combine flour and sugar. In a large jug whisk together buttermilk, eggs, butter and vanilla in a large jug. Gradually whisk egg mixture into flour mixture until batter is smooth. Stand for 30 minutes. Reserve 6 strawberries for later. Cut remaining strawberries into thin slices.
step 2 Preheat a frying pan. Spray with oil. Pour ¼ cup batter into pan. Arrange about 3 strawberry slices on top. Cook for 1-2 minutes, until bubbles form on the surface. Turn and cook for 1 minute. Repeat with remaining batter and strawberries.
step 3 Serve in stacks of 3 pancakes. Top with reserved strawberries and dust with icing sugar. Serve with yogurt, cream or ice-cream, if desired.

tips Other berries may be used. Prepare batter in a blender or with a hand blender if preferred. These pancakes freeze well.

pancakes with maple cream

makes 12
preparation 10 minutes (plus standing time)
cooking 20 minutes

2 cups (300g) plain flour
3 teaspoons baking powder
2 tablespoons caster sugar
1½ cups (375 ml) milk
2 eggs, lightly beaten
60g butter, melted, cooled, plus extra for cooking
2 bananas, thinly sliced
maple cream
250g packet cream cheese, at room temperature
½ cup (125ml) maple syrup, plus extra to serve
1 teaspoon ground cinnamon

step 1 Sift flour and baking powder into a large bowl. Add sugar.
Whisk milk, eggs and butter together. Make a well in the centre
of the flour. Gradually blend in milk mixture until smooth. Stand
for 15 minutes.
step 2 maple cream: In a small bowl beat cream cheese using an
electric mixer, until smooth. Slowly beat in syrup and cinnamon.
step 3 Heat a large non-stick frying pan on medium heat. Brush
pan with a little extra butter. Pour ⅓ cup measures of batter into
pan, tilting pan to make a circle. Cook for 2-3 minutes until
bubbles start to appear on surface. Turn and cook for a further
1 minute until golden. Transfer to a plate and cover to keep warm.
Repeat with remaining batter. Serve pancakes topped with maple
cream and banana slices. Drizzle with extra maple syrup.

cheesy breakfast rolls

makes 6
preparation 10 minutes
cooking 15 minutes

2 cups (300g) self-raising flour
30g butter
1 cup (120g) grated cheddar cheese
¾ cup (67g) rolled oats
½ cup (125ml) milk + ½ cup (125ml) water
1 tablespoon snipped chives

step 1 Preheat oven to very hot, 220°C. Lightly grease a baking tray. Sift flour into a bowl. Add butter. Using fingertips, lightly rub in until mixture is combined. Mix in ½ cup (60g) cheese and ½ cup (45g) oats. Make a well in centre.
step 2 In a jug, combine the milk and water. Pour into the well all at once, reserving 1 tablespoon of liquid. Using a palette knife, quickly mix to a soft, sticky dough. Do not over-mix. Turn onto a lightly floured work surface. Knead lightly. Divide dough into 6 even-sized pieces.
step 3 Lightly knead each piece into a ball, pressing out slightly. Place close together on prepared tray. Brush rolls with reserved milk mixture. In a bowl, combine remaining cheese, remaining oats and chives. Sprinkle over rolls. Bake for 12-15 minutes until rolls sound hollow when tapped. Allow to cool on a wire rack.

ham & cheese scrolls

makes about 10
preparation 10 minutes
cooking 15 minutes

2 cups (300g) self-raising flour
30g butter, chopped
3 tablespoons chopped basil
½ cup (125ml) milk + ½ cup (125ml) water
1 cup (120g) grated cheddar cheese
½ cup (100g) chopped ham
½ red pepper, deseeded, chopped
¼ cup (30g) chopped gherkin (optional)

step 1 Preheat oven to very hot, 220°C. Lightly grease a baking tray.

step 2 Sift flour into a large bowl. Add butter. Using fingertips, rub in lightly. Stir in basil.

step 3 Make a well in the centre of flour mixture. Pour in combined milk and water all at once, reserving 1 tablespoon. Using a palette knife, mix quickly to a soft, sticky dough. Do not over-mix.

step 4 Turn onto a lightly floured surface. Knead lightly. Press or roll out to form a rectangle about 1cm thick.

step 5 In a small bowl, combine cheese, ham, capsicum and gherkin, if using. Sprinkle over dough, pressing slightly.

step 6 Roll into a log shape. Cut into 2cm-thick slices and arrange cut side up, slightly overlapping, on baking tray. Brush with reserved milk mixture. Bake for 12-15 minutes until scrolls sound hollow when tapped. Transfer to a wire rack. Allow to cool.

choc-chip pikelets

makes about 20
preparation 5 minutes
cooking 10 minutes

1 cup (150g) self-raising flour
½ cup (95g) chocolate chips
2 tablespoons caster sugar
1 cup (250ml) milk
1 egg
65g butter, melted
whipped cream, to serve

step 1 Sift flour into a bowl. Stir in chocolate chips and sugar.
step 2 In a jug, whisk together milk, egg and 50g butter until combined. Gradually add to flour mixture, whisking until smooth.
step 3 Heat a large non-stick frying pan on medium heat. Brush with a little of the remaining melted butter.
step 4 Drop level tablespoonfuls of batter into pan and cook for 1-2 minutes, until bubbles appear on the surface. Turn and cook the other side for 1 minute or until golden.
step 5 Repeat with remaining batter, brushing the pan with butter between batches. Serve pikelets with cream.

tip As the pikelets are made with self-raising flour, there's no need to rest the batter before you cook them.

breakfast pizzas

serves 4
preparation 10 minutes
cooking 15 minutes

2 round ciabatta rolls, halved horizontally
⅓ cup (80ml) barbecue sauce
2 tomatoes, sliced
4 eggs
1 cup (120g) grated mozzarella cheese
6 rashers rindless bacon, quartered
rocket leaves, to serve

step 1 Preheat oven to hot, 200°C. Line a baking tray with foil. Spread each half of the rolls with barbecue sauce.
step 2 Arrange tomato slices around the edge of each half. Break an egg into the centre of each half roll and sprinkle evenly with mozzarella cheese. Season to taste. Bake for 10-15 minutes until egg-white is set.
step 3 Meanwhile, heat a frying pan on high and fry bacon for 1-2 minutes each side, until crispy. Top pizzas with bacon and season to taste. Serve with rocket leaves.

tip Instead of bacon, you can use prosciutto or ham.

19

snacks & light lunches

tomato, pumpkin & rocket pizza 22
beefy pies 25
courgette fritters with guacamole 26
chicken bolognese pasta pots 29
jacket potatoes with baked beans 30
butternut squash soup 33
salami, tomato & cheese melts 34
mini hot dogs 37
lemonade floats 37
ribbon sandwich 38

tomato, pumpkin & rocket pizza

makes 2
preparation 15 minutes
cooking 45 minutes

500g pumpkin (or butternut squash),
    peeled, cubed
1 tablespoon olive oil
2 sheets frozen shortcrust pastry, thawed
½ cup (125ml) tomato pasta sauce
1 cup (120g) grated mozzarella cheese
200g cherry tomatoes
1 red pepper, deseeded, finely chopped
40g baby rocket leaves

step 1 Preheat oven to hot, 200°C. Toss
pumpkin with oil in a baking tray. Bake for
25-30 minutes until tender. Set aside.
step 2 Meanwhile, halfway through cooking
pumpkin, lightly grease 2 baking trays. Cut a
20cm round from each pastry sheet. Place on
prepared trays. Prick pastry with a fork and
bake for 10 minutes.
step 3 Spread each pastry round with tomato
pasta sauce. Sprinkle with half the cheese.
Top with tomatoes, pepper and pumpkin.
Sprinkle with remaining cheese. Bake for
10-15 minutes until golden and the bases are
crisp. Top with rocket. Serve in wedges.

beefy mini pies

makes 24 mini pies
preparation 35 minutes
cooking 45 minutes, plus chilling time

1 tablespoon vegetable oil
3 rashers rindless bacon, finely
  chopped
1 onion, finely chopped
750g minced beef
⅓ cup (50g) plain flour
2½ cups (625ml) beef stock
1 tablespoon tomato paste

1 teaspoon chopped rosemary
6 sheets frozen shortcrust
  pastry, thawed
3 sheets frozen puff pastry,
  thawed
1 egg, lightly beaten
¼ cup (75g) sesame seeds
tomato sauce, to serve

step 1 Preheat oven to hot, 200°C. Lightly grease 2 x 12-hole
muffin trays. Heat oil in a large saucepan on high. Sauté bacon
and onion for 3-4 minutes until onion is tender. Add mince and
brown well for 4-5 minutes.

step 2 Blend in flour and cook, stirring, for 1 minute. Gradually
stir in stock, tomato paste and rosemary and bring to the boil,
stirring. Reduce heat and simmer, uncovered, for 10 minutes or
until mixture reduces and thickens. Transfer to a large bowl.
Cool for 10 minutes and then chill in fridge until cold.

step 3 Meanwhile, using a 10cm cutter, cut 24 rounds of
shortcrust pastry. Ease into each tray hole. Using an 8cm cutter,
cut 24 rounds of puff pastry. Spoon 2 tablespoons filling into
each shell and brush edges with a little egg. Top each pie with
puff pastry rounds, pressing edges to seal. Brush with egg and
sprinkle with sesame seeds. Bake for 20-25 minutes or until
golden and puffed. Rest in tray for 5 minutes. Serve with sauce.

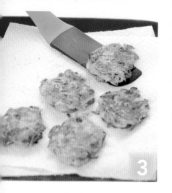

courgette fritters with guacamole

makes about 16
preparation 15 minutes
cooking 25 minutes

2 courgettes, grated
½ cup (60g) frozen peas
½ cup (60g) grated cheddar cheese
⅓ cup (50g) flour, sifted
2 eggs, lightly beaten
1 tablespoon vegetable oil
guacamole, to serve (see note)

step 1 In a medium bowl, combine courgettes, peas, cheese, flour and eggs. Season to taste.
step 2 Heat oil in a large frying pan on medium. Cook tablespoonfuls of mixture in 4 batches for 2-3 minutes each side until golden.
step 3 Drain fritters on paper towel. Top each fritter with 1 teaspoon of guacamole to serve.

note To make guacamole, combine 1 peeled and stoned avocado and ¼ cup (60ml) low-fat soured cream in a bowl. Season to taste.

chicken bolognese pasta pots

makes 6
preparation 20 minutes
cooking 25 minutes

1½ cups (270g) macaroni or other short pasta
1 tablespoon olive oil
500g minced chicken
400g can diced tomatoes
375g jar tomato pasta sauce
100g button mushrooms, thinly sliced
2 tablespoons chopped basil
⅓ cup (50g) grated parmesan
⅓ cup (40g) grated cheddar cheese

step 1 Grease 6 x 1-cup ramekins.
step 2 Cook pasta in a saucepan of boiling, salted water for 8-10 minutes until al dente. Drain well.
step 3 Meanwhile, heat oil in a medium saucepan on high. Add minced chicken. Cook for 5-6 minutes, breaking up lumps with back of a spoon as it browns. Add diced tomatoes, tomato pasta sauce and mushroom. Simmer for 10 minutes. Stir in basil and season to taste. Stir through pasta until combined.
step 4 Divide mixture evenly between ramekins. In a bowl, combine parmesan and tasty cheese. Sprinkle over pasta pots.
step 5 Preheat grill to high. Place ramekins on a baking tray. Grill for 2-3 minutes until cheese melts and is golden. Serve.

jacket potatoes with baked beans

serves 4
preparation 15 minutes
cooking 30 minutes

4 large potatoes, scrubbed
¼ cup (50g) finely chopped salami or
   cabanossi
¼ cup (30g) grated cheddar cheese
2 teaspoons snipped chives
200g can baked beans

step 1 Preheat oven to moderate, 180°C.
Lightly grease a baking tray. Pierce potatoes in
several places with a skewer. Arrange on
turntable of microwave oven. Cook on high
(100%) power for 12-14 minutes until tender.
step 2 Meanwhile, in a small bowl, combine
salami, cheese and chives. Cut a small slice off
base of each potato so they sit flat. Using a
teaspoon, scoop out 1cm of potato centre.
step 3 Chop excess potato and mix with
salami mixture. Place potatoes on prepared tray.
Spoon an even amount of baked beans into
each potato. Top with salami mixture. Bake for
10-15 minutes until topping is crispy.

tip You can also cook the filled potatoes in the
microwave on HIGH (100%) for 2 minutes.

butternut squash soup

serves 4-6
preparation 15 minutes
cooking 30 minutes

1 tablespoon olive oil
2 onions, chopped
2 garlic cloves, crushed
½ butternut squash, peeled, deseeded,
  chopped
1 potato, peeled, chopped
1 litre vegetable or chicken stock
½ cup (125ml) milk
cream, snipped chives, crusty bread to serve

step 1 Heat oil in a large saucepan on high.
Sauté onion and garlic for 2-3 minutes until
onion is tender. Add squash and potato.
Cook, stirring for 1 minute.
step 2 Pour over stock. Bring to boil. Simmer
covered for 15-20 minutes until the vegetables
are very tender.
step 3 Puree mixture using a hand blender
(or transfer to a food processor). Stir in milk.
Reheat gently. Serve with a swirl of cream.
Garnish with a sprinkling of chives. Serve
with crusty bread.

salami, tomato & cheese melts

makes 4
preparation 5 minutes
cooking 5 minutes

2 English muffins, halved
2 tablespoons tomato paste
4 slices salami, chopped
½ small red pepper, deseeded, finely chopped
⅓ cup (40g) grated mozzarella or cheddar cheese

step 1 Preheat grill to medium. Line a baking tray with foil. Place muffin halves, cut-side up, on tray.
step 2 Grill for 1 minute each side until lightly toasted.
step 3 Spread tomato paste over muffin halves. Top with salami, pepper and cheese.
step 4 Grill for 3-4 minutes until cheese melts and is golden.

tip Vary the ingredients – try canned pineapple rings, ham and cheese, barbecued chicken, mushroom and cheese.

mini hot dogs

makes 6
preparation 5 minutes
cooking 10 minutes

6 pack part-baked bread rolls
6 cocktail hot dog sausages (pre-cooked)
⅓ cup (40g) grated cheddar cheese
tomato sauce, to serve

step 1 Preheat oven to hot, 200°C. Lightly grease and line a
baking tray.
step 2 Slit each roll through the top, being careful not to cut
all the way through.
step 3 Place a sausage in each roll. Sprinkle with cheese. Bake
for 5-10 minutes until the cheese melts and sausages are hot.
Serve with tomato sauce and lemonade floats (see below).

lemonade floats

serves 6
preparation 5 minutes

6 large scoops vanilla ice-cream
1.5 litres lemonade

step 1 Place a scoop of ice-cream into each glass.
Divide lemonade between glasses and serve straightaway.

tip You can use any type of fizzy drink you like.

ribbon sandwich

serves 1
preparation 10 minutes

2 tablespoons mayonnaise
2 teaspoons chopped basil
3 thick slices high-fibre bread
1 tablespoon redcurrant jelly
1 slice skinless turkey breast
1 slice cheddar cheese
¼ cup (10g) mustard and cress
1 lettuce leaf
1 slice lean ham
1 small tomato, sliced

step 1 In a small bowl, combine mayonnaise and basil. Set aside. Spread 1 slice of bread with redcurrant jelly and top with turkey, cheese and cress. Place another slice of bread on top.
step 2 Spread the second slice of bread with mayonnaise mixture, then top with the lettuce leaf, ham and tomato. Finish with the last piece of bread.
step 3 Cut the sandwich into 3 fingers and wrap firmly in cling film. Store in the fridge until required.

tip Cover any leftover mayonnaise and basil mixture and store in an airtight container in the fridge.

desserts

pavlova parfait

serves 6
preparation 10 minutes

2 punnets strawberries, hulled, chopped
2 tablespoons icing sugar
600ml carton whipping cream, whipped
1 punnet raspberries
100g packet meringue nests, lightly crushed
2 chocolate Flakes, lightly crushed

step 1 Combine strawberries and icing sugar in a large bowl. Mash lightly and set aside for 10 minutes.
step 2 Fold through the cream, raspberries and crushed meringue.
step 3 Spoon into 6 serving glasses. Sprinkle with Flake. Serve immediately.

tip This is also a great way of using a meringue case that has collapsed.

chocolate caramel puddings

makes 4
preparation 20 minutes
cooking 35 minutes

1 cup (150g) self-raising flour
¼ cup (25g) cocoa powder
¾ cup (165g) caster sugar
½ cup (125ml) skimmed milk
1 egg, lightly beaten
30g low-fat spread, melted
⅓ cup (40g) chopped soft caramels
2 tablespoons brown sugar
1 tablespoon chopped pecans
ice-cream, to serve

step 1 Preheat oven to moderate, 180°C. Brush 4 x 1-cup ramekins lightly with oil.

step 2 Sift flour and cocoa together into a large bowl. Stir in sugar. Blend in milk, egg and melted spread. Fold in caramels.

step 3 Spoon mixture into prepared ramekins. Sprinkle with combined brown sugar and pecans. Place ramekins in a baking tin. Pour enough hot water to come halfway up the sides of dishes. Bake for 30-35 minutes until cooked when tested. Serve warm with ice-cream.

tip Puddings are cooked when a skewer inserted into pudding comes out clean and dry.

choc-chip bread & butter pudding

serves 6
preparation 15 minutes (plus standing time)
cooking 30 minutes

6 slices white bread
2 tablespoons spreadable butter
2 x 375ml cans evaporated milk
3 eggs
⅓ cup (75g) caster sugar
1 teaspoon vanilla extract
⅓ cup (65g) chocolate chips
extra thick double cream, to serve

step 1 Preheat oven to moderate, 180°C.
Lightly grease a 6-cup ovenproof dish. Spread
each slice of bread with butter. Cut bread into
quarters, diagonally. Arrange the bread pieces
in the prepared dish, slightly overlapping.
step 2 In a large jug, whisk together the milk,
eggs, sugar and vanilla. Stir in choc chips. Pour
over the bread in the dish. Stand for 10 minutes
until some of the mixture has been absorbed.
step 3 Place dish in a large baking tin and add
enough boiling water to the tin so it comes
halfway up the sides of the dish (this is called a
'water bath'). Bake for 25-30 minutes, until
custard is just set. Cool for 5 minutes before
serving with thick cream.

chocolate pancakes with chocolate custard

serves 4-6
preparation 15 minutes (plus standing time)
cooking 30 minutes

2 cups (300g) self-raising flour
2 tablespoons cocoa powder
⅓ cup (75g) caster sugar
600ml buttermilk
2 eggs, lightly beaten
50g butter, melted
spray cooking oil
raspberries and grated
   chocolate, to serve

chocolate custard
2 egg-yolks
¼ cup (55g) caster sugar
2 tablespoons cornflour
¾ cup (180ml) milk
½ cup (125ml) double
   cream
100g dark chocolate,
   melted

step 1 Sift flour and cocoa into a large bowl. Stir in sugar. Whisk in combined milk, eggs and butter. Stand for 30 minutes.

step 2 chocolate custard: Meanwhile, in a medium bowl, whisk egg-yolks, sugar and cornflour together. Bring combined milk and cream to the boil in a saucepan on medium. Remove from heat. Gradually whisk in to egg-yolk mixture. Return custard mixture to saucepan. Stir in chocolate. Heat, stirring constantly, on low until mixture thickens and coats the back of a spoon. Do not boil. Remove custard from heat.

step 3 Spray a large frying pan with oil and heat on medium. Cook ¼-cup measures of pancake mixture for 2-3 minutes, until bubbles form on surface. Turn and cook for a further 2 minutes. Repeat with remaining batter, spraying pan with oil as required. Serve warm pancakes drizzled with chocolate custard. Sprinkle with raspberries and grated chocolate.

rice pudding with caramelised pears

serves 4-6
preparation 15 minutes
cooking 1 hour 30 minutes

15g butter, melted
2 cups (500ml) milk
300ml double cream
¼ cup (30g) short-grain rice
¼ cup (55g) caster sugar
1 teaspoon vanilla extract
¼ teaspoon ground nutmeg
caramelised pears
30g butter
4 medium pears, peeled, cored, thickly sliced
½ cup (110g) brown sugar
¼ cup (120ml) double cream

step 1 Preheat oven to moderately low, 160°C. Brush a deep, 6-cup casserole dish liberally with melted butter. Combine all ingredients in dish. Bake, covered, for 1 hour until rice is creamy and almost tender, stirring occasionally.
step 2 Remove lid. Stir and cook further 30 minutes, uncovered, adding more milk as required.
step 3 caramelised pears: Meanwhile, melt butter in a pan over medium heat until foaming. Add the pears and cook, stirring occasionally, for 4-5 minutes until tender and golden. Blend in sugar and cream and cook for 2-3 minutes, stirring occasionally, until sauce thickens slightly. Serve pudding topped with pears.

fruit kebab dippers

makes 12
preparation 20 minutes
cooking 1 minute

12 strawberries, hulled
2 kiwi fruit, peeled
2 slices pineapple, peeled
2 small bananas, peeled
¼ small cantaloupe melon, deseeded, peeled
12 coloured straws
¼ cup (85g) chocolate hazelnut spread
¼ cup (90g) honey
3 tablespoons hundreds and thousands

step 1 Chop fruit into even-sized chunks and thread onto the straws.
step 2 Place the chocolate hazelnut spread and honey in separate microwave-safe bowls. Heat each in the microwave on medium (50%) power for 20 seconds or until runny.
step 3 Pour hundreds and thousands onto a plate, dip and coat fruit kebabs in desired toppings.

tip Try serving the fruit kebabs with chocolate sprinkles and desiccated coconut as well as hundreds and thousands.

raspberry & mango ice-pops

makes 8
preparation 10 minutes, plus freezing time

1 cup (150g) frozen raspberries
1 cup (250ml) lemonade
4 frozen mango cheeks, chopped
1 cup (250ml) orange juice
8 lolly-pop sticks

step 1 Place the raspberries and lemonade in a blender and blend until smooth. Pour into 8 x 200ml ice-block moulds. Freeze for 30 minutes until partially frozen.
step 2 Place mango and orange juice in a blender and blend until smooth. Pour over raspberry mixture. Insert a lolly-pop stick in the centre of each. Continue to freeze overnight until firm.

tip To remove moulds, dip them into warm water for a few seconds.

baking

jam tarts

makes 24
preparation 20 minutes
cooking 10 minutes

4 sheets frozen shortcrust pastry, thawed
1 egg white
1 tablespoon sugar
¼ cup (80g) raspberry jam
¼ cup (80g) orange marmalade
¼ cup (80g) plum jam
¼ cup (80g) lime marmalade
small decorative pastry cutters

step 1 Preheat oven to moderate, 180°C.
Lightly grease 2 x 12-hole shallow bun tins.
Cut 24 x 6.5cm rounds from pastry. Press into
prepared recesses.

step 2 Cut remaining pastry using small
decorative pastry cutters. Place on baking
parchment-lined tray. Brush with egg-white.
Sprinkle with sugar.

step 3 Bake tart cases and pastry shapes for
8-10 minutes until golden. Spoon 2 teaspoons
jam into tart cases. Top with shapes.

tip Use any jam, marmalade or curd you prefer.

chocolate custard & strawberry tarts

makes 8
preparation 20 minutes (plus chilling time)
cooking 30 minutes

2 sheets frozen shortcrust pastry, thawed
⅓ cup (50g) custard powder
1 tablespoon cocoa powder
150ml milk
150ml boiling water
200g sweetened condensed milk
1 teaspoon vanilla extract
8 strawberries, hulled, quartered

step 1 Preheat oven to hot, 200°C. Lightly grease 8 holes of a
12-hole muffin tray. Cut 8 x 12cm rounds from pastry and press
into tray holes. Cover each pastry case with baking parchment,
fill with uncooked rice or dried beans, then bake blind for
10 minutes. Remove rice or beans and paper, then bake for a
further 10 minutes. Set aside to cool.

step 2 Combine custard powder and cocoa in a bowl. Stir in
enough milk to form a paste. Heat remaining milk and water in a
saucepan on low until warm. Blend milk into custard and return
to saucepan. Cook, stirring, for 4-5 minutes or until custard boils
and thickens slightly. Simmer for a further 3 minutes.

step 3 Stir in condensed milk and vanilla. Remove from heat and
set aside to cool. Cover and chill until cold. Fill tart cases with
chocolate custard and top with strawberries.

honey jumbles

makes 20
preparation 20 minutes, plus chilling time
cooking 10 minutes

⅓ cup (115g) honey
45g butter
1 cup (150g) plain flour
1 teaspoon ground ginger
½ teaspoon mixed spice
½ teaspoon bicarbonate
  of soda

¼ teaspoon ground cloves
1 tablespoon milk
icing
1 egg white
1½ cups (240g) icing sugar,
  sifted
few drops pink food colouring

step 1 In a small saucepan, heat honey and butter together on low until melted and simmering. Allow to cool for 5 minutes.
step 2 Sift flour, ginger, mixed spice, bicarbonate of soda and cloves together into a bowl. Make a well in the centre. Pour in honey mixture and milk. Stir until well combined. Cover with cling film and chill for 30 minutes or until firm.
step 3 Preheat oven to moderate, 180°C. Line two baking trays with baking parchment.
step 4 Turn dough onto a lightly floured surface. Knead, gradually working in a little extra flour, if needed, until the dough is no longer sticky.
step 5 Divide into 2 pieces. Roll each into a sausage shape about 4cm thick. Cut into 5mm widths. Arrange on trays. Press into oval shapes. Bake for 8-10 minutes until they begin to crack. Cool on trays.
step 6 icing: Place egg white in a bowl. Whisk until frothy. Gradually add icing sugar, blending until smooth. Stir in colouring. Spread evenly over biscuits. Allow to become firm.

star biscuits

makes about 20
preparation 20 minutes (plus chilling time)
cooking 12 minutes

125g butter, chopped at room temperature
½ cup (110g) caster sugar
1 teaspoon vanilla extract
1 egg
2 cups (300g) plain flour
1 teaspoon baking powder
milk for glazing
coloured sugar for decorating

step 1 Preheat oven to moderate, 180°C.
Lightly grease 2 large baking trays. In a small
bowl, using an electric mixer, beat butter, sugar
and vanilla. Beat in egg until combined. Add
sifted flour and baking powder. Place onto a
floured board. Knead lightly until combined.
Wrap in cling film and chill for 30 minutes.

step 2 Roll dough between 2 sheets of baking
parchment until 0.5cm thick. Using an 8cm star
cutter, cut shapes from dough. Place onto
prepared tray.

step 3 Brush with milk and sprinkle lightly with
coloured sugar. Bake for 10-12 minutes, or until
golden. Cool on trays.

muesli crispie bars

makes 16
preparation 10 minutes, plus chilling time
cooking 5 minutes

50g butter
250g packet marshmallows
2 cups (70g) Rice Krispies™
¾ cup (70g) rolled oats
½ cup (35g) shredded coconut
½ cup (75g) dried cranberries
⅓ cup (80g) pepitas (see tip)

step 1 Lightly grease an 18 x 28cm slice tin. Line base and sides with baking parchment.

step 2 In a medium saucepan, combine butter and marsh-mallows. Heat on low for 5-6 minutes, stirring, until melted and smooth.

step 3 In a large bowl, combine remaining ingredients. Add marshmallow mixture. Working quickly, mix well and press into prepared pan. Using a wet spatula, flatten top.

step 4 Chill for 2-3 hours until firm. While still in pan, cut into bars. You can store in an airtight container in the fridge for up to 1 week.

tip Pepitas are edible pumpkin seeds that have had their white hull removed. They are·green with a delicate nutty flavour.

mango & coconut muffins

makes 12
preparation 10 minutes
cooking 25 minutes

2½ cups (375g) self-raising flour, sifted
425g can mango in natural juice, drained,
  chopped
1 cup (80g) desiccated coconut
¾ cup (165g) caster sugar
1¼ cups (310ml) buttermilk
185g reduced-fat spread, melted
1 egg, lightly beaten
1 cup (40g) Special K™, lightly crushed

step 1 Preheat oven to moderate, 180°C.
Lightly spray a 12-hole muffin tray with oil. In a
large bowl, combine flour, mango, coconut and
sugar. In a jug, mix buttermilk, spread and egg.

step 2 Make a well in centre of the dry
ingredients. Add buttermilk mixture all at once.
Mix lightly, until just combined (see tip).
step 3 Spoon mixture evenly into recesses in
prepared tray. Sprinkle with Special K. Bake
20-25 minutes, until cooked when tested. Cool
in tray 5 minutes. Transfer to a wire rack to cool.

tips Sixteen strokes is usually enough when
mixing muffin batter – any pockets of flour help
to give them their characteristic texture.

sultana cupcakes with lemon icing

makes 12
preparation 15 minutes
cooking 25 minutes

125g butter, at room
  temperature, chopped
⅔ cup (150g) caster sugar
1 teaspoon vanilla extract
2 eggs
¾ cup (110g) self-raising flour,
  sifted

⅔ cup (165ml) milk
¾ cup (120g) sultanas
sugar flowers, to decorate
lemon glace icing
2 cups (320g) icing sugar
15g softened butter
1-2 tablespoons lemon juice

step 1 Preheat oven to moderate, 180°C. Line a 12-hole muffin tray with paper cake cases. In a bowl, using an electric mixer, cream butter and sugar together until light and fluffy. Beat in the vanilla extract. Add eggs, one at a time, beating well after each addition.

step 2 Fold in flour alternately with milk, beginning and ending with flour. Fold in sultanas. Spoon mixture into paper cases until two-thirds full.

step 3 Bake for 20-25 minutes or until cooked when tested with a skewer. Cool in tray for 5 minutes before turning onto a wire rack to cool completely.

step 4 lemon glace icing: Sift icing sugar into a bowl. Beat in butter and enough lemon juice to make icing a smooth, spreadable consistency. Spread evenly over cakes. Top with sugar flowers.

butterfly cakes

makes 12
preparation 20 minutes
cooking 25 minutes

125g butter, at room temperature, chopped
⅔ cup (150g) caster sugar
1 teaspoon vanilla extract
2 eggs
1¾ cups (260g) self-raising flour, sifted
⅔ cup (165ml) milk
300ml whipping cream, whipped
sliced strawberries, coloured sugar, to decorate (optional)
icing sugar, to dust

step 1 Preheat oven to moderate, 180°C. Line a 12-hole muffin
tray with paper cake cases. In a large bowl, using an electric
mixer, cream butter and sugar together until light and fluffy.
Beat in vanilla extract.
step 2 Add eggs, one at a time, beating well after each
addition. Fold in flour alternately with milk, beginning and
ending with flour. Spoon mixture into paper cases until two-thirds
full. Bake for 20-25 minutes or until a skewer inserted in the
centre comes out clean and dry. Cool in tray for 5 minutes.
Transfer to a wire rack to cool completely.
step 3 Using a sharp knife, cut a circle from the top of each
cake. Slice in half to make wings. Fill cavities with cream.
Top cakes with wings and decorate with strawberry slices and
coloured sugar, if using. Dust with icing sugar to serve.

simple iced chocolate cake

serves 12
preparation 15 minutes
cooking 40 minutes

60g butter
¾ cup (165g) caster sugar
1 egg
1½ cups (225g) self-raising
   flour
2 tablespoons cocoa powder
½ cup (125ml) milk

¼ cup (60ml) boiling water
¼ teaspoon bicarbonate
   of soda
chocolate icing
1 cup (160g) icing sugar
1 tablespoon cocoa powder
1-2 tablespoons boiling water

step 1 Preheat oven to moderate, 180°C. Lightly grease a deep 20cm round cake tin and line base with baking parchment. In a bowl, using an electric mixer, beat butter and sugar until smooth and creamy. Add egg, beating well.

step 2 Sift flour and cocoa together, well. Fold into creamed mixture alternately with milk, beginning and ending with flour mixture. In a jug combine water and soda. Lightly fold into mixture. Spread into prepared tin. Bake for 35-40 minutes or until a skewer inserted into the centre comes out clean and dry. Cool in tin for 5 minutes. Transfer to a wire rack to cool completely.

step 3 chocolate icing: In a bowl, sift icing sugar and cocoa together well. Blend water into icing sugar mixture until smooth. Spread over cold cake.

tip Store cake in an airtight container for up to 5 days or wrap in cling film and freeze for up to 2 months.

iced finger buns

makes 9
preparation 10 minutes
cooking 15 minutes

2 cups (300g) self-raising flour
30g butter, chopped
¼ cup (40g) sultanas
2 tablespoons sugar
¾ cup (180ml) milk
1 egg
1 tablespoon just-boiled water

1 tablespoon caster sugar
icing
1 cup (160g) icing sugar, sifted
1 tablespoon just boiled water
1 teaspoon butter
few drops pink food colouring

step 1 Preheat oven to very hot, 220°C. Grease a baking tray.
step 2 Sift flour into a bowl. Add butter. Using fingertips, lightly rub in until well combined. Stir in sultanas and sugar.
step 3 Make a well in the centre of flour mixture. In a jug, whisk together milk and egg. Pour into well all at once, reserving 1 tablespoon. Using a palette knife, quickly mix to a soft, sticky dough. Do not over-mix.
step 4 Turn onto a lightly floured surface. Knead lightly. Break dough into 9 even-sized pieces. Roll into finger-bun shapes.
step 5 Place buns close together on prepared tray. Brush with reserved milk mixture. Bake for 12-15 minutes until buns sound hollow when tapped. Remove from oven.
step 6 In a jug, combine water and caster sugar. Brush over buns. Transfer to a wire rack. Allow to cool.
step 7 icing: In a bowl, combine icing sugar, water and butter. Add food colouring. Mix well. Spread on buns. Serve with or without butter.

glossary

baking powder raising agent mostly containing cream of tartar and bicarbonate of soda in the proportions of 1 teaspoon cream of tartar to ½ teaspoon bicarbonate of soda (equal to 2 teaspoons baking powder).

barbecue sauce a spicy, tomato-based sauce used to marinate, baste or as an accompaniment.

basil an aromatic herb; there are many types, but the most commonly used is sweet basil.

bicarbonate of soda also called baking soda.

brioche rich French yeast-risen bread made with butter and eggs.

buttermilk fresh low-fat milk cultured to give a slightly sour, tangy taste; low-fat yogurt or milk can be substituted.

button mushrooms small, cultivated white mushrooms with a delicate, subtle flavour.

cheese

cheddar the most common cow's milk cheese; should be aged and hard.

mozzarella a semi-soft cheese with a delicate, fresh taste; has a low melting point and stringy texture when hot.

parmesan a sharp-tasting, dry, hard cheese, made from skimmed or semi-skimmed milk and aged for at least a year.

chives related to the onion and leek, with subtle onion flavour.

ciabatta meaning 'slipper' in Italian, the traditional shape of this popular crisp-crusted white bread.

cinnamon dried inner bark of the shoots of the cinnamon tree. Also available ground.

coconut

desiccated unsweetened and concentrated, dried finely shredded coconut.

shredded thin strips of dried coconut.

cornflour also known as cornstarch; used as a thickening agent in cooking.

cream

soured a thick commercially-cultured soured cream.

whipping commercially thickened cream.

custard powder instant mixture used to make pouring custard.

flour

plain all-purpose flour.

self-raising plain flour with baking powder (a raising agent consisting mainly of 2 parts cream of tartar to 1 part bicarbonate of soda) in the proportion of 150g flour to 2 level teaspoons baking powder.

gherkin also known as cornichon; young, dark-green cucumbers grown for pickling.

ginger also known as green or root ginger; the thick gnarled root of a tropical plant.

maple syrup distilled from the sap of maple trees found only in Canada and parts of North America. Maple-flavoured syrup is not an adequate substitute for the real thing.

milk

condensed a canned product consisting of milk with more than half the water content removed and sugar added.

evaporated an unsweetened canned milk concentrated by evaporation.

skimmed we used skimmed milk with 0.1g fat per 100ml.

mixed spice a blend of ground spices usually consisting of cinnamon, allspice and nutmeg.

muffin, English or breakfast muffin, is a round, yeast-leavened form of bread baked on a griddle.

nutmeg dried nut of an evergreen tree; available in ground form or you can grate your own with a fine grater.

oil

olive mono-unsaturated; made from the pressing of tree-ripened olives. Extra virgin and virgin are the best, obtained from the first pressings of the olive, while extra light or light refers to the taste, not fat levels.

vegetable any number of oils sourced from plants rather than animal fats.

pecans native to the United States; golden-brown, buttery and rich.

pumpkin also known as squash; a member of the gourd family and used as an ingredient or eaten on its own. Various types can be substituted for one another.

rocket also known as arugula, rugula and rucola; a peppery-tasting green leaf.

rolled oats traditional whole oat grains that have been steamed and flattened. Not the quick-cook variety.

sesame seeds black and white are the most common of these tiny oval seeds; a good source of calcium.

sugar

brown an extremely soft, fine granulated sugar retaining molasses for its deep colour and flavour.

caster also known as superfine or finely granulated table sugar.

icing also known as confectioners' sugar or powdered sugar.

tomato paste triple-concentrated tomato puree used to flavour soups, stews, sauces and casseroles.

conversion charts

MEASURES

The cup and spoon measurements used in this book are metric: one measuring cup holds approximately 250ml; one metric tablespoon holds 20ml; one metric teaspoon holds 5ml.

All cup and spoon measurements are level.

The most accurate way of measuring dry ingredients is to weigh them. When measuring liquids, use a clear glass or plastic jug with metric markings.

We use large eggs with an average weight of 60g.

warning This book may contain recipes for dishes made with raw or lightly cooked eggs. These should be avoided by vulnerable people such as pregnant and nursing mothers, invalids, the elderly, babies and young children.

DRY MEASURES

METRIC	IMPERIAL
15g	½oz
30g	1oz
60g	2oz
90g	3oz
125g	4oz (¼lb)
155g	5oz
185g	6oz
220g	7oz
250g	8oz (½lb)
280g	9oz
315g	10oz
345g	11oz
375g	12oz (¾lb)
410g	13oz
440g	14oz
470g	15oz
500g	16oz (1lb)
750g	24oz (1½lb)
1kg	32oz (2lb)

LIQUID MEASURES

METRIC	IMPERIAL
30ml	1 fl oz
60ml	2 fl oz
100ml	3 fl oz
125ml	4 fl oz
150ml	5 fl oz (¼ pint/1 gill)
190ml	6 fl oz
250ml	8 fl oz
300ml	10 fl oz (½ pint)
500ml	16 fl oz
600ml	20 fl oz (1 pint)
1000ml (1 litre)	1¾ pints

LENGTH MEASURES

METRIC	IMPERIAL
3mm	⅛in
6mm	¼in
1cm	½in
2cm	¾in
2.5cm	1in
5cm	2in
6cm	2½in
8cm	3in
10cm	4in
13cm	5in
15cm	6in
18cm	7in
20cm	8in
23cm	9in
25cm	10in
28cm	11in
30cm	12in (1ft)

OVEN TEMPERATURES

These oven temperatures are only a guide for conventional ovens. For fan-assisted ovens, check the manufacturer's manual.

	°C (CELSIUS)	°F (FAHRENHEIT)	GAS MARK
Very low	120	250	½
Low	150	275–300	1–2
Moderately low	160	325	3
Moderate	180	350–375	4–5
Moderately hot	200	400	6
Hot	220	425–450	7–8
Very hot	240	475	9

index